CRAFT ATTACK!

JEWELLERY CRAFTS

Annalees Lim

W

FRANKLIN WATTS

LONDON • SYDNEY

First published in 2014 by Franklin Watts

Copyright © 2014 Arcturus Publishing Limited

Franklin Watts
338 Euston Road
London NW1 3BH

Franklin Watts Australia
Level 17/207 Kent Street, Sydney NSW 2000

Produced by Arcturus Publishing Limited,
26/27 Bickels Yard, 151–153 Bermondsey Street, London SE1 3HA

The right of Annalees Lim to be identified as the author of this work has been asserted by her in accordance with the Copyright, Designs and Patents Act 1988.

Editors: Joe Harris and Sara Gerlings
Designer: Elaine Wilkinson
Cover design: Elaine Wilkinson
Photography: Simon Pask

A CIP catalogue record for this book is available from the British Library.

Dewey Decimal Classification Number 745.5'942
ISBN 978 1 4451 2933 4

Printed in China

Franklin Watts is a division of Hachette Children's Books, an Hachette UK company.

www.hachette.co.uk

SL003835UK
Supplier 03, Date 0114, Print Run 3032

CONTENTS

MAKE YOUR OWN JEWELLERY

You'll always stand out from the crowd with handmade jewellery and accessories. All the projects in this book are easy to follow, but that doesn't mean that the final pieces won't make a big impact. You can look a million dollars, while saving a fortune!

Everyday Treasures

You don't have to rush down to your local craft shop before getting started. First have a look around at what you already have. You might have odd buttons from old clothes that you could use, a broken bead necklace that could be recycled or a spare ribbon.

Shop Around

There are lots of places where you can find materials for your jewellery. Try looking in hardware stores for round washers, rings or hooks. Second-hand shops will have lots of cheap jewellery that you can reuse the clasps and fastenings from.

Keep It Clean!

If you buy second-hand earrings, it's important that you clean them thoroughly before wearing them. Ask an adult to help you with this. First leave them to soak in boiling water for a few minutes. Then remove them, dry them and wipe them with some surgical spirit.

Jewellery Wire and Wire Cutters

Jewellery wire is very flexible, easy to cut and comes in different thicknesses and colours. To cut it you will need wire cutters, a piece of specialist equipment that professional jewellery makers use. In this book we use a pair of round-nose wire cutters. Ask an adult to help when you are using wire cutters.

Cloth Tape Measure

You don't always need to be precise when you are making jewellery, but it's good to have a tape measure to hand in case you want two pieces to be identical.

Clasps and Fastenings

Jewellery fastenings normally come in two parts and help you to take your jewellery on and off easily. You can buy them new from craft shops, or you may decide you want to recycle old jewellery.

PVA Glue

A crafts essential! This sticks most things together and can be used to make papier mâché.

Fabric Glue

This is brilliant for sticking paper or card to (yes, you guessed it!) fabric.

Craft Glue

This is useful if you need to stick metal or plastic things (such as buttons or googly eyes) to your crafts.

Superglue

This is a very strong kind of glue, and should only be used with adult supervision.

PENDANT NECKLACE

Pendants are jewels or other trinkets that hang from a chain. They can be made from many different objects. Believe it or not, this pendant is made from metal washers!

Pendants can also be used on earrings. You could make a matching pair!

You will need
Embroidery thread
Metal washers (3 small, 1 medium and 1 large)
An old chain
Scissors

1 Tie a piece of embroidery thread to a small metal washer and start wrapping the thread round and round. Keep wrapping until you have covered the whole washer. Then repeat this twice more with other small washers.

2 Tie the three small washers together with embroidery thread of a different colour, so that they form a small triangle.

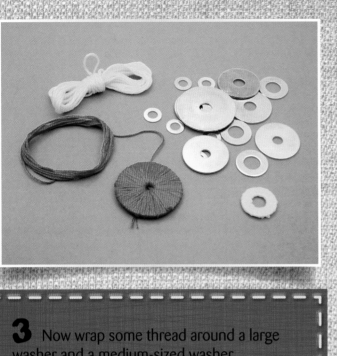

3 Now wrap some thread around a large washer and a medium-sized washer.

4 Attach the triangle of small washers to the large washer using more embroidery thread. Then attach the medium-sized washer to the other side.

5 Thread your chain through the hole in the medium-sized washer.

LUCKY RABBIT EARRINGS

Aren't these bunny earrings cute? You can make them for pierced or unpierced ears. Remember to ask an adult to help you when using wire cutters.

You will need

Jewellery wire
Wire cutters
Small, medium and large beads
Small pom-pom
Scissors
Felt and fabric glue
Earring hooks or clips
Tape measure

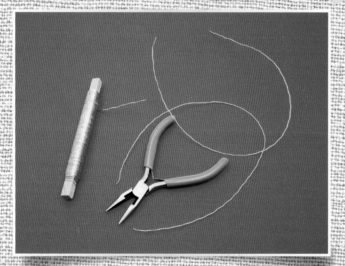

1 Cut two lengths of jewellery wire 40 cm (15 in) long, using wire cutters

2 Thread one medium-sized bead to the middle of each wire and twist the wire to hold it in place. This will be the rabbit's head.

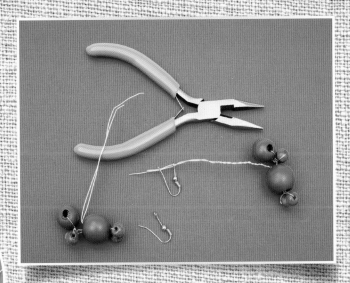

3 Thread a small bead onto both ends of each wire. Slide the beads down. Twist the ends of the wire together just above them. Push both ends of the wire through a large bead (the body). Then slide down two more small beads and twist again.

4 Poke the wires back through the bead body. Attach the earring hook or clip to the wire, and snip off any spare wire.

5 Cut out four small felt ears. Use fabric glue to stick them to the rabbits' heads. Finally, glue a small pom-pom to the back of each earring. This is the tail!

It was once believed that a rabbit's foot could bring you luck. Now that you're wearing eight, you should be especially lucky!

BRILLIANT BEAD BRACELET

Why not make your own beads? It's fun and easy, and you can create lots of different pieces of jewellery. Here's how you can make a bracelet.

You will need
Polymer clay
Elastic and scissors
Clay tools (optional)
Wooden toothpick

1 Choose three pieces of polymer clay in different colours. Warm them in your hands to make them soft.

2 Mix all three colours together so they make a marbled effect. Don't mix them too much or they will become murky.

3 Break off small pieces of clay and roll them into round beads. You will need about 10 to 12 beads in total. Make sure you have enough to go around your wrist. Make a hole in each of the beads, using the toothpick.

4 Make a small butterfly out of another piece of polymer clay. Clay tools will help with this. Press the butterfly onto one of your beads. Ask an adult to help you bake all of your polymer clay pieces in the oven, as directed on the packet.

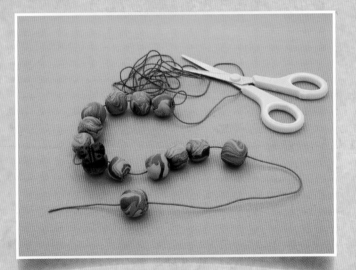

5 Once the clay has completely cooled, string the beads onto a piece of elastic. Tie a knot in the elastic and cut off the loose ends.

KNOTTED BRACELET

Sailors' knots are very useful to know if you are sailing the open seas. But did you ever think about using them to make a fashion bracelet? Take your time with the figure-eight knots – don't get yourself in a tangle!

You will need
String or shoelace 40 cm (15 in) long
Jewellery clasps
Wire cutters
Beads
Scissors

1 Half the string should be free, and half bundled up. Holding the bundled end, loop the free string into a backwards 'c'.

2 Keeping hold of the bundled end, lead the string up and over itself to make a 'b'.

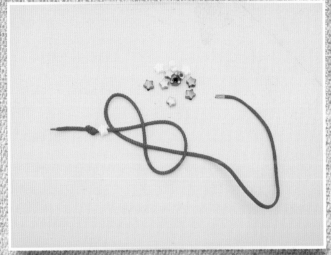

3 Bring the string back downwards but this time lead it under the straight line. This will make a figure '8' shape.

4 Pass the string through the bottom loop of the '8': first over, then under. Pull it tight.

5 Repeat steps 1–4 to make more knots. Slide a bead onto the string at the bottom of each new knot. Do this all along the string. Tighten the knots carefully, pulling at either end to make sure they are in the right place.

6 Measure the knotted string against your wrist and trim it down if necessary. Then ask an adult to help you use wire cutters to attach some clasps to each end.

COOL COLLAR NECKLACE

Collar necklaces are wide, chunky pieces of jewellery. They are a great way to make a bold statement!

You will need

Patterned and coloured paper
Cardboard
Hole punch
Chain
Pen and paintbrush
Scissors
PVA glue

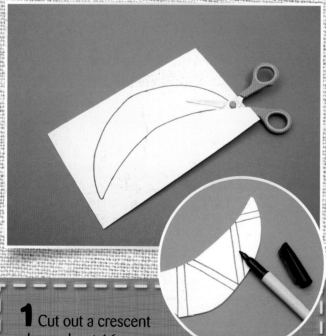

1 Cut out a crescent shape about 16 cm (6 in) long from your cardboard. Draw on some simple shapes.

2 Tear up some patterned paper into small pieces.

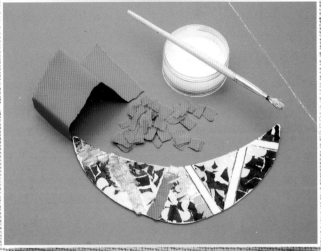

3 Use PVA glue to stick torn-up paper over most of your design. Leave some details (such as stripes or spots) uncovered.

4 Tear up more paper in a contrasting colour. Glue it over the uncovered spaces. Coat the whole thing with a layer of PVA glue and leave it to dry.

5 Punch a hole in either end of the collar, then thread it onto your chain.

FABRIC FLOWER RING

A large, colourful ring can really transform an outfit. Why not make several fabric rings in different colours to match different outfit choices, or to give to friends?

You will need

Felt
Scissors
Old ring
Needle and thread
Craft glue
Fabric glue
Button

1 Cut out five petal shapes from felt, about 3 cm (1 in) long. Then cut out five smaller petal shapes in a different colour.

2 Pinch together the bottom of each petal. Ask an adult to help you sew a few stitches into each petal so that it stays pinched.

3 Ask your adult assistant to help you stitch the five large petals together in the centre. Do the same with the smaller petals.

4 Glue the two sets of petals together in the centre with fabric glue. Leave to dry.

5 Use the craft glue to fix a big button to the middle of the flower. Leave to dry. With adult help, sew the flower to your old ring.

You could attach these cute fabric flowers to other things, such as bags, tops, hats or brooch pins.

FRIENDS FOREVER NECKLACES

These two bird necklaces are perfect for sharing with one of your friends. You keep one and they have the other to remind you both of the great fun and laughs you have together.

You will need

Leather thread
Aluminium foil
Stick-on gems
2 hooks
Glue stick, craft glue and glitter glue
Scissors
Pen and card

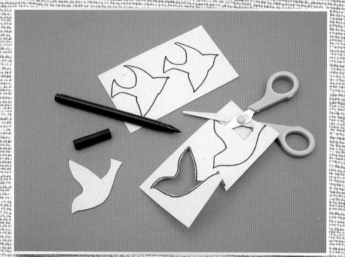

1 Cut out four bird shapes from card. You will need two identical pairs. An easy way to make a matching pair is to trace around the first bird to make the second one.

2 Place your birds on aluminium foil, making sure the identical birds are facing in opposite directions. Cut roughly around them, so the foil shape is bigger than the card. Stick the card down with a glue stick. Wrap the foil edges around the card.

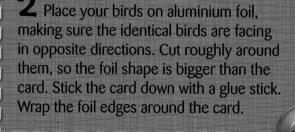

3 Place a hook in the middle of each pair of birds. Glue them together with the hook in the middle, using craft glue. Leave to dry.

4 Add some details with glitter glue, and use stick-on gems for eyes. Leave to dry.

5 Add a leather thread to each of the hooks.

SEW EASY FELT BROOCH

Brooches are a kind of jewellery that you pin to your clothes. They can really jazz up plain tops or coats! This apple tree brooch is easy to make but looks super-cool.

You will need

Felt
Brooch pin
Needle and thread
Pins
Paper
Pen
Scissors

1 Draw an apple tree onto a piece of paper.

2 Cut around the whole design with scissors. Pin it to a piece of felt, and cut the felt to the same shape.

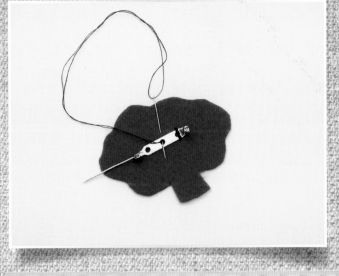

3 Follow the same method for each of the smaller shapes that make up the apple tree. Cut around the shapes on paper, pin them to felt and then cut the felt to the same shape.

4 Ask an adult to help you sew your brooch together. First, stitch the brooch pin onto the back of the tree outline shape.

5 Sew all the small shapes – the apples, leaves, trunk and stems – onto the tree canopy shape. Use a simple stitch around the edges. Why not use brightly coloured thread? Finally, stitch the tree canopy and trunk shapes to the tree outline shape.

Why not start with an apple tree, then try making other designs from your own imagination? The possibilities are endless!

FUNKY TOY HAIR CLIPS

Do you have any old, unwanted plastic toys hiding at the back of your bedroom cupboards? Here's a fun way to turn them into cute and quirky jewellery. You won't be able to find hair clips like these in the shops!

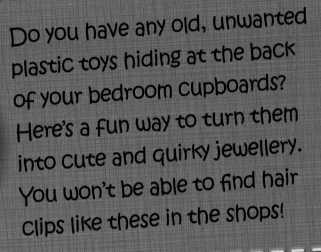

1 Collect together some items you want to attach to your clips and clean them so they are free of dirt and dust.

2 When they are completely dry, paint each one a different colour using acrylic paint.

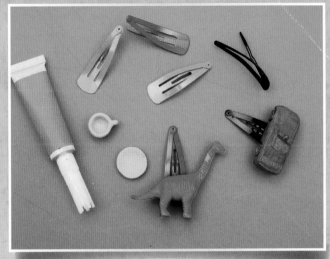

3 When the paint has dried, cover the toys with a thin layer of PVA glue. This will give them a shiny finish.

4 Ask an adult to superglue each toy to a clip. Leave the glue to set.

5 Use craft glue to attach some small beads onto the toys.

JEWELLED CUFF

Cuffs are much wider than normal bracelets. This means that you have a nice large space to fill with colours and patterns! You could use a cuff like this as part of an outfit for a fancy dress party.

You will need
Cardboard tube
Craft foam shapes
Stick-on gems
Craft glue
Metallic paint
Scissors

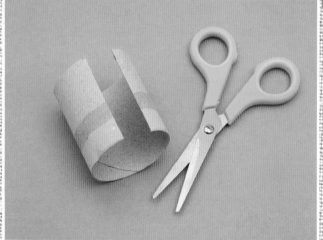

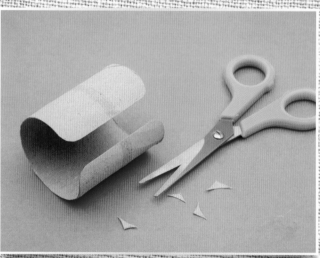

1 Cut a 6-cm (2-in) section from your cardboard tube with scissors. Snip down the length of the section so that you can get the cuff on and off your wrist.

2 Cut around the edges of each corner using your scissors.

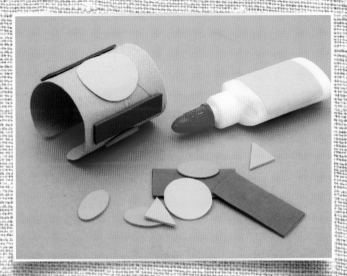

3 Use craft glue to decorate the cuff with craft foam shapes.

4 Paint the whole cuff with metallic paint and leave it to dry.

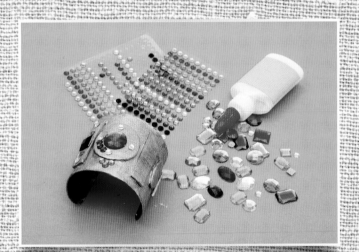

5 Decorate your cuff with some stick-on gems.

Alternatively, you could decorate your cuff with a collage.

PUZZLE PIECE HAIR COMB

Hair combs look great in long or short hair, and they can brighten up any outfit! These hair combs may look puzzling, but all your friends will love them.

You will need
Old puzzle pieces
Acrylic paint
Needle and thread
Paintbrush
Plain hair comb
Ribbon
Craft glue
Scissors
Tape measure

1 Choose three pieces from an old puzzle. Make sure that nobody wants to use it again!

2 Paint each piece in a different colour, using your acrylic paint.

3 Cut a length of ribbon 30 cm (12 in) long. Fold it back and forth into a concertina. Ask an adult to pass a needle through the middle of the ribbon, then fan it out like a flower. Fix it in place with a few stitches.

4 Make two more ribbon 'flowers'. Use craft glue to stick the puzzle pieces to them.

5 Fix the puzzle pieces and ribbon onto the hair comb with the craft glue. Leave to dry.

BUTTON BAG CHARM

Your favourite bag can be made even more stylish with a colourful charm. This can be attached anywhere: for example on handles, zips or loops. You could make one for each of your bags.

You will need

Beads
Small and large buttons
Wire
Wire cutters
Key ring clasp
Tape measure

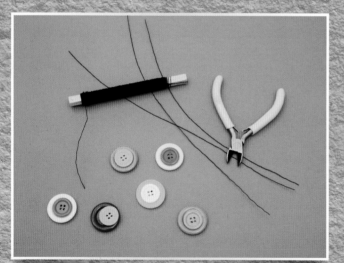

1 Place six small buttons onto six large buttons, making sure that the holes line up. Cut three pieces of wire 30 cm (12 in) long.

2 Thread a wire through one of the button stacks from underneath, into one hole and out of another. It will hold the buttons together. Thread two wires together in and out of the other two buttonholes.

3 Thread the other five button stacks onto five of the wires attached to the first button. One wire should be left free.

4 Curl the wires behind the buttons so that they are fixed firmly in place. Thread some chunky beads onto the last remaining free wire.

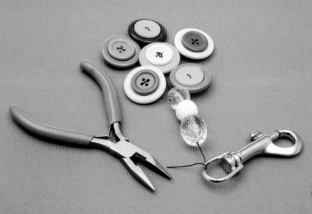

5 Attach the key ring clasp to the wire loop.

JEWELLERY TREE

Now that you have made all this awesome jewellery, you will want somewhere to display it! That's where this nifty tree comes in...

You will need

Gardening wire
Acrylic paint
Cardboard
Paintbrush
Wire cutters
Masking tape
Scissors
Pen or pencil
Ruler

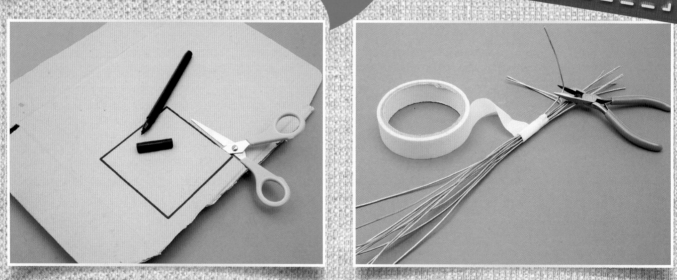

1 Cut a 10 x 10 cm (4 x 4 in) base from cardboard, using scissors.

2 Ask an adult to help you cut ten 30-cm (12-in) lengths of wire, using wire cutters. Ask the adult to gather the wire together in a bunch and secure it in place about 6 cm (2.5 in) from one end with some masking tape.

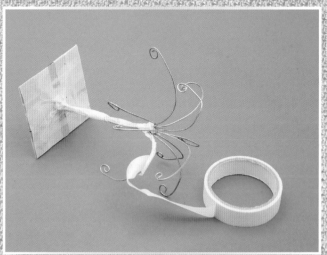

3 Spread out the wires at the shorter end and secure them to the base with masking tape. Spread out the free ends of the wires to make branches. Ask an adult to help you curl the very ends with wire cutters.

4 Cover the whole tree with masking tape, including the base.

5 Paint the jewellery tree in acrylic paint and leave it to dry. When it has dried, you can hang your jewellery on the tree!

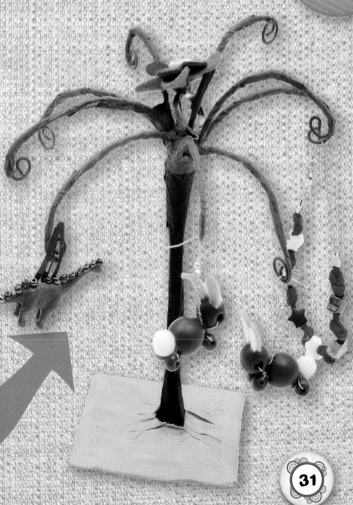

GLOSSARY

acrylic paint A type of fast-drying paint, available in bright colours.

concertina fold Continuous folding that results in a zigzag shape.

crescent A shape that resembles a new moon.

polymer clay A type of manmade modelling clay used for making arts and crafts items.

surgical spirit A type of rubbing alcohol used as an antiseptic and cleanser.

washer A small metal ring used in plumbing.

FURTHER READING

How to Improve at Making Jewellery by Sue McMillan (TickTock Books, 2010)

Jewellery by Laura Torres (QED Publishing, 2013)

Jewellery Crafting for Kids by Sarah Fiorenza (Ryland Peters & Small, 2012)

WEBSITES

http://spoonful.com/crafts
Crafts and activities for a range of ages.

http://www.education.com/activity/beads-jewelry/
Bead and jewellery crafts for children.

http://www.allfreejewelrymaking.com/
Free jewellery and bead patterns.

INDEX

SERIES CONTENTS

Jewellery Crafts
Make Your Own Jewellery • Pendant Necklace • Lucky Rabbit Earrings • Brilliant Bead Bracelet • Knotted Bracelet • Cool Collar Necklace • Fabric Flower Ring • Friends Forever Necklaces • Sew Easy Felt Brooch • Funky Toy Hair Clips • Jewelled Cuff • Puzzle Piece Hair Comb • Button Bag Charm • Jewellery Tree

Nature Crafts
Going Wild with Nature Crafts • Woodland Photo Frame • Painted Pebble Plant Pot • Butterfly Bunting • Sand Art • Shell Creature Fridge Magnets • Pressed Flower Coasters • Leafy Bird Mobile • Seed Mosaic • Japanese Blossom Tree • Pebble Zoo • Brilliant Bird Box • Pine Cone Field Mouse • Lavender Hand Warmers

Paper Crafts
Getting Crafty with Paper • Cube Puzzle • Pop-Up Painting • Paper Planets • Paper Pulp Monsters • Make Your Own Notebook • Secret Seashell Storage Box • 3-D Photo Art • Quilling Cards • Giant Crayons • Paper Globe Lampshade • Paper Cup Disco Ball • Envelopes and Notepaper • Paper Bouquet

Printing Crafts
Perfect Printing • Apple Print Canvas Bag • Block Printed Cards • One-Off Portrait Print • Funky Pattern Prints • Stencil Art Plant Pot • Clay Printing • Roller Print Folders • Cling Film Wrapping Paper • Button Print Trainers • Easy Screen Prints • Spotty Painted Mugs • Bubble Print T-Shirt • Sandpaper Printing

Recycling Crafts
Crafty Recycling • Jam Jar Lanterns • Bottle Tops in Bloom • Funny Face Vase • Stackable Rocket Boxes • Beach Hut Pen Pots • Bedroom Pinboard • Water Bottle Bracelets • Scrap Paper Daisy Chain • Peacock Bookends • Sunny Days Clock • Starry Sky Mail Mobile • CD Case Photo Frame • Plastic Bag Weaving

Textile Crafts
Terrific Textiles • Cute Sock Owls • Rock Star Rag Doll • Toadstool Doorstop • Funky Felt Friend • Cocoa Cosy • Totally Brilliant Tote • Awesome Accessories • Jean Genius Desk Mascot • Secret Diary Cover • Mini Bag Organizer • Cupcake Pincushion • Knitted Phone Case